THE WORLD'S BIGGEST
MAMMALS

by Mari Schuh

pogo

Ideas for Parents and Teachers

Pogo Books let children practice reading informational text while introducing them to nonfiction features such as headings, labels, sidebars, maps, and diagrams, as well as a table of contents, glossary, and index.

Carefully leveled text with a strong photo match offers early fluent readers the support they need to succeed.

Before Reading

- "Walk" through the book and point out the various nonfiction features. Ask the student what purpose each feature serves.
- Look at the glossary together. Read and discuss the words.

Read the Book

- Have the child read the book independently.
- Invite him or her to list questions that arise from reading.

After Reading

- Discuss the child's questions. Talk about how he or she might find answers to those questions.
- Prompt the child to think more. Ask: What is the biggest mammal you have ever seen?

Pogo Books are published by Jump!
5357 Penn Avenue South
Minneapolis, MN 55419
www.jumplibrary.com

Copyright © 2016 Jump!
International copyright reserved in all countries.
No part of this book may be reproduced in any form without written permission from the publisher.

Library of Congress Cataloging-in-Publication Data

Schuh, Mari C., 1975- author.
  The world's biggest mammals / by Mari Schuh.
      pages cm — (The world's biggest animals)
  Audience: Ages 7-10.
  Includes index.
  ISBN 978-1-62031-204-9 (hardcover: alk. paper) –
  ISBN 978-1-62031-257-5 (paperback) –
  ISBN 978-1-62496-291-2 (ebook)
  1. Mammals–Size–Juvenile literature.
  2. Body size–Juvenile literature. I. Title.
  QL706.2.S337 2016
  599–dc23
                                                      2014045515

Series Editor: Jenny Fretland VanVoorst
Series Designer: Anna Peterson
Photo Researcher: Anna Peterson

Photo Credits: All photos by Shutterstock except: Christopher Swann/SeaPics.com, 14; David B. Fleetham/SeaPics.com, 18-19; Nature Picture Library, 1, 8-9; Thinkstock, 4, 6.

Printed in the United States of America at Corporate Graphics in North Mankato, Minnesota.

TABLE OF CONTENTS

CHAPTER 1
What Are Mammals?........................4

CHAPTER 2
Largest on Land............................6

CHAPTER 3
Big Blue.................................14

ACTIVITIES & TOOLS
How Heavy?.............................22
Try This!...............................23
Glossary...............................23
Index..................................24
To Learn More.........................24

WHAT ARE MAMMALS?

A mother chimpanzee **grooms** her baby.

A baby pig drinks its mother's milk.

What do these animals have in common?

They are both **mammals**. Mammals have hair or fur. They feed milk to their young.

Cats, dogs, and cows are mammals. You are a mammal, too!

LARGEST ON LAND

Elephants are the world's largest land mammals.

They can weigh up to 15,000 pounds (6,800 kilograms). That is more than four cars!

Because elephants are so big, they need lots of food. They spend most of the day eating.

Elephants can eat more than 300 pounds (136 kg) of food in just one day.

They use their long trunk like a hand. They eat grass, roots, bark, and fruit.

DID YOU KNOW?

There are two kinds of elephants. African elephants are bigger than Asian elephants.

African Elephant

Asian Elephant

trunk

Female elephants usually give birth to one calf at a time.

Calves weigh more than 200 pounds (91 kg) at birth. They are already heavier than many human adults.

Calves drink their mother's milk. In their first year, they gain up to three pounds (1.3 kg) a day. They are full-grown at about 10 years.

DID YOU KNOW?

An elephant's tooth is the size of a brick.

Each tooth weighs four pounds (1.8 kg) or more.

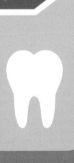

calf

WHERE ARE THEY?

Elephants roam the land in Africa and Asia. They live in **grasslands**, deserts, forests, and **swamps**. They live together in small family groups.

AFRICA & ASIA

■ = Elephant Range

Elephants may be largest on land. But they are tiny when compared to the blue whale.

A full-grown elephant still only weighs as much as a blue whale's tongue.

CHAPTER 3

BIG BLUE

Blue whales are huge.

They are, in fact, the biggest animals that have ever lived.

Blue whales can weigh more than 300,000 pounds (136,000 kg).

They can be nearly 100 feet (30 meters) long. That is longer than two school buses.

Can you imagine that?

DID YOU KNOW?

Apatosaurus was one of the biggest dinosaurs to walk the earth.

A blue whale weighs more than four of these dinosaurs.

Blue whales are born big. A blue whale calf weighs more than a minivan.

Each day, it drinks 50 gallons (189 liters) of milk from its mother. As it grows, it gains 200 pounds (91 kg) a day.

calf · · · · ▶

Blue whales are huge, but the food they eat is tiny. They swallow thousands of **krill** in one big gulp.

A blue whale can eat 8,000 pounds (3,600 kg) of krill in one day.

WHERE ARE THEY?

Elephants roam the land in Africa and Asia. They live in **grasslands**, deserts, forests, and **swamps**. They live together in small family groups.

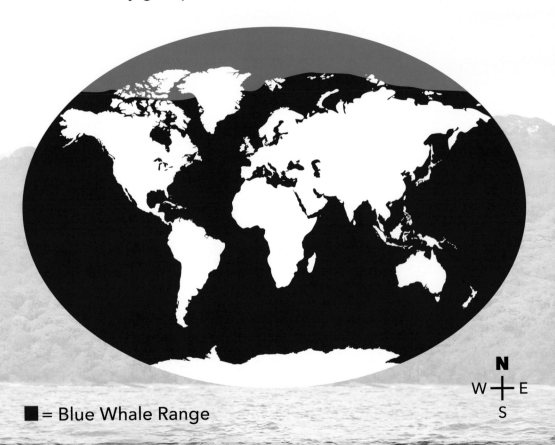

■ = Blue Whale Range

N
W ╋ E
S

Huge blue whales glide through the ocean. Powerful elephants stride across the land. On land and at sea, mammals are the biggest animals in the world.

What is the biggest mammal you've ever seen?

ACTIVITIES & TOOLS

HOW HEAVY?

A blue whale can weigh as much as 20 African elephants.
An African elephant can weigh as much as 300 second graders!

Weigh a family pet. Have an adult help you. Then weigh your backpack, a big toy, or a bag of sugar. Does it weigh more than your pet?

· ·

GLOSSARY

blood vessel: A tube that carries blood throughout the body.

grassland: Land covered with grasses rather than shrubs and trees.

groom: To clean and take care of.

krill: A small animal that is like a shrimp.

mammal: A warm-blooded animal that breathes air and has hair or fur; female mammals make milk to feed to their young.

mate: To join together to produce young.

migrate: To regularly move from one place to another.

ocean: A large body of salt water.

swamp: Wet, muddy, spongy land often partly covered with water.

INDEX

Africa 12

Asia 12

blue whale 13, 14, 15, 16-17, 18-19, 20-21

calves 10, 18

dinosaur 16

eating 8, 19

elephant 6, 7, 8-9, 10-11, 12-13, 21

food 8, 19

fur 5

hair 5

heart 19

krill 19

length 16

mammals 5, 6

mating 20

migrating 20

milk 4, 5, 10, 18

ocean 20, 21

tooth 10

trunk 8

weight 7, 8, 10, 16, 18, 19

TO LEARN MORE

Learning more is as easy as 1, 2, 3.

1) Go to www.factsurfer.com

2) Enter "biggestmammals" into the search box.

3) Click the "Surf" to see a list of websites.

With factsurfer, finding more information is just a click away.